Weston Intermediate School
95 School Road
Weston, CT 06883

Weston Intermediate School
95 School Road
Weston, CT 06883

THE WILD WORLD OF ANIMALS

THE WILD WORLD OF ANIMALS

SWANS

MARY HOFF

CREATIVE EDUCATION

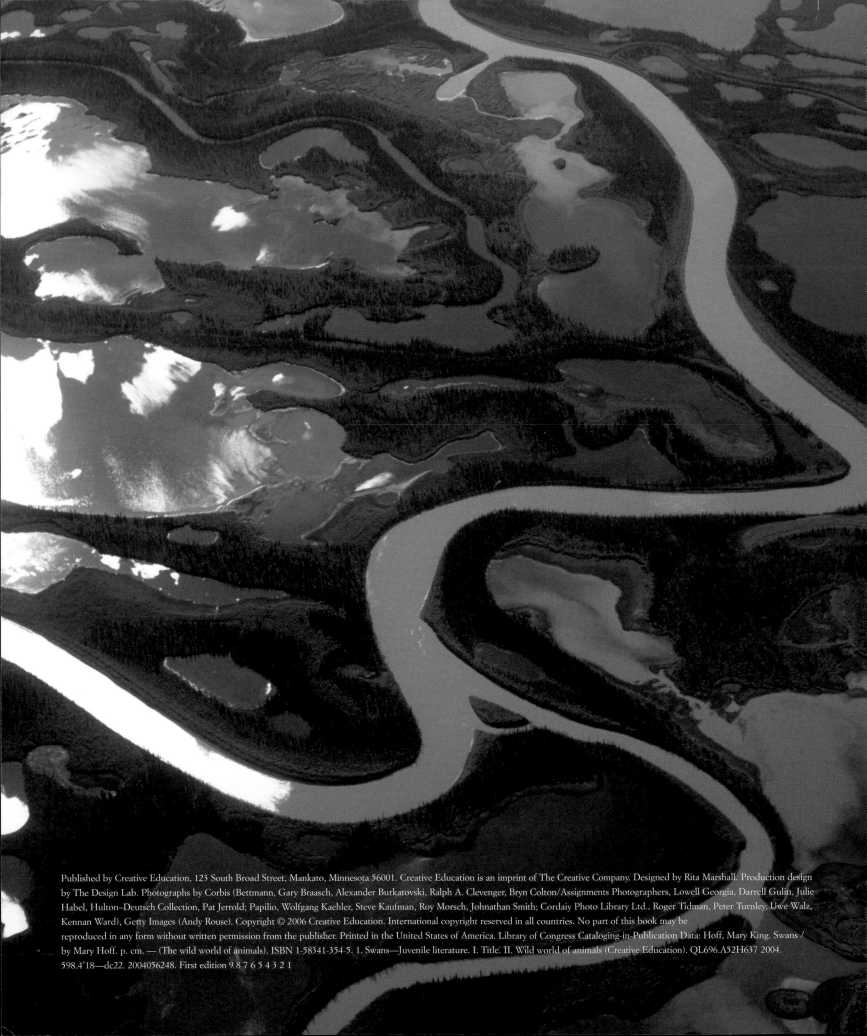

Published by Creative Education, 123 South Broad Street, Mankato, Minnesota 56001. Creative Education is an imprint of The Creative Company. Designed by Rita Marshall. Production design by The Design Lab. Photographs by Corbis (Bettmann, Gary Braasch, Alexander Burkatovski, Ralph A. Clevenger, Bryn Colton/Assignments Photographers, Lowell Georgia, Darrell Gulin, Julie Habel, Hulton–Deutsch Collection, Pat Jerrold; Papilio, Wolfgang Kaehler, Steve Kaufman, Roy Morsch, Johnathan Smith; Cordaiy Photo Library Ltd., Roger Tidman, Peter Turnley, Uwe Walz, Kennan Ward), Getty Images (Andy Rouse). Copyright © 2006 Creative Education. International copyright reserved in all countries. No part of this book may be reproduced in any form without written permission from the publisher. Printed in the United States of America. Library of Congress Cataloging-in-Publication Data: Hoff, Mary King. Swans / by Mary Hoff. p. cm. — (The wild world of animals). ISBN 1-58341-354-5. 1. Swans—Juvenile literature. I. Title. II. Wild world of animals (Creative Education). QL696.A52H637 2004. 598.4'18—dc22. 2004056248. First edition 9 8 7 6 5 4 3 2 1

It's a crisp October morning on the Mackenzie River in northern Canada. As the sun rises, its golden light reveals hundreds of huge, white birds. Some are resting on land. Others are swimming on the river. Still others are taking off or landing. These are tundra swans. After spending the summer near the Arctic Circle, they are getting ready for their fall migration. The swans will soon fly to the eastern coast of the United States. There they will winter in wetlands near the ocean. When spring comes, they will fly north once again.

Swans reflect natural beauty and grace **5**

FLOATING AND FLYING

Tundra swans are one of seven kinds of swans in the world. The other types of swans are black, black-necked, coscoroba, mute, trumpeter, and whooper swans. Most swans are a dazzling white, but some are black. All swans have long necks. Their bills are long and **tapered** when seen from the side.

6 Tundra swans can fly as high as 10,000 feet (3,050 m)

Swans are among the largest flying birds on Earth. The tundra swan is a medium-sized swan. It weighs about 14 pounds (6 kg)—10 times as much as a wild duck. Each wing is about 20 inches (50 cm) long. With their necks outstretched, tundra swans can measure more than four feet (1.2 m) from the end of their bill to the tips of their tail feathers.

Tundra swans are **migratory** birds. In the summer, they nest near the Arctic Circle in North America, Asia, and Europe. In the fall, they fly south to the eastern and western coasts of the United States and to European and Asian countries such as Great Britain, the Netherlands, China, and Japan. No matter where they are, swans like to be near water.

Some swans travel thousands of miles **9**

Swans have many **adaptations** that help them survive in their summer and winter homes and on the long flight in between. A swan uses its webbed feet to paddle around in search of underwater plants to eat. Its long, flexible neck allows the swan to reach down to uproot the plants. A swan's bill has hairlike structures called "lamellae" around the edges. The lamellae help it grab plants. They also act as a strainer so the swan can squeeze water out of its mouth without losing the food it has gathered.

Some swans' necks are as long as their bodies   **11**

More than 25,000 feathers cover a swan's body. They help keep the swan warm and dry, even in water. Oil is produced by a structure called a "preen gland," which is located near the tail feathers. Swans use their bills to spread the oil on their feathers, helping to make them waterproof.

Swans' bodies are good for flying as well as floating. The shape of their bodies helps air flow smoothly past them. Their huge wings carry them through the air. Like other birds, swans have hollow bones. The bones are strong but weigh less than solid bones—a good **trait** for animals that fly!

Swans take excellent care of their thick feathers   **13**

Because tundra swans live in so many places, they have many kinds of animal neighbors. In their summer homes, they may see arctic foxes, grizzly bears, and ravens. Their winter neighbors include snow geese in America and whooper swans in Europe.

Swans live near grizzly bears (opposite) and ravens (above) **15**

LIFE AS A SWAN

Splash! Water sprays in all directions as two tundra swans land on a lake in northern Russia. It's spring, and these swans have just completed the journey from their wintering grounds in Great Britain. They are mates,

Male and female swans look alike

which means they live together and raise
young together. Like other swan pairs, they
will stay together until one of them dies.

The two swans gather moss, grass, and
other plants. They build a nest five feet
(1.5 m) in **diameter** near a lake or pond.
The female, called a "pen," lays four eggs
in the nest. She sits on the eggs, warming
them with her body. The male, called a
"cob," stays nearby, guarding the nest
from **predators** such as gulls, coyotes,
eagles, and foxes.

If one swan dies, the other may find a new mate   **17**

After about a month, the eggs hatch. The young swans, called "cygnets," have grayish **down**. They weigh about six ounces (170 g) and have pink bills. They can swim soon after hatching.

18 Male swans are very protective of their mates and young

At first, the cygnets eat tiny animals found in the water. As they grow, they begin to eat mainly plants. They learn to fly two or three months after they hatch.

Cygnets don't turn white until they are about a year old   **19**

While the cygnets are growing, the adult swans molt, discarding their old feathers and growing new ones, just as people get new clothes when their old ones wear out. Then, in late summer, the swans gather with other swan families for the long journey south. When they finally set off, they travel in "V" formations, often a half-mile (800 m) or more above the ground. Swans can fly faster than a car drives on the freeway. That's good, because they have a long way to travel. Some tundra swans fly almost 4,000 miles (6,440 km) to their winter homes!

When migrating, swans stop near water to rest

As they fly, tundra swans make sounds. They call with a "hoo-hoo" sound, like a goose. The wind in their wings makes a whistling sound. Other kinds of swans make sounds like trumpets or bugles.

When they arrive at their winter homes, tundra swans again live near water. In addition to eating underwater plants, they now also eat shellfish and bits of plants left in fields after crops have been harvested.

Tundra swans make the journey from north to south every year throughout their lives. They can live a long time. One wild tundra swan in Europe lived more than 25 years!

Whooper swans like these make loud sounds

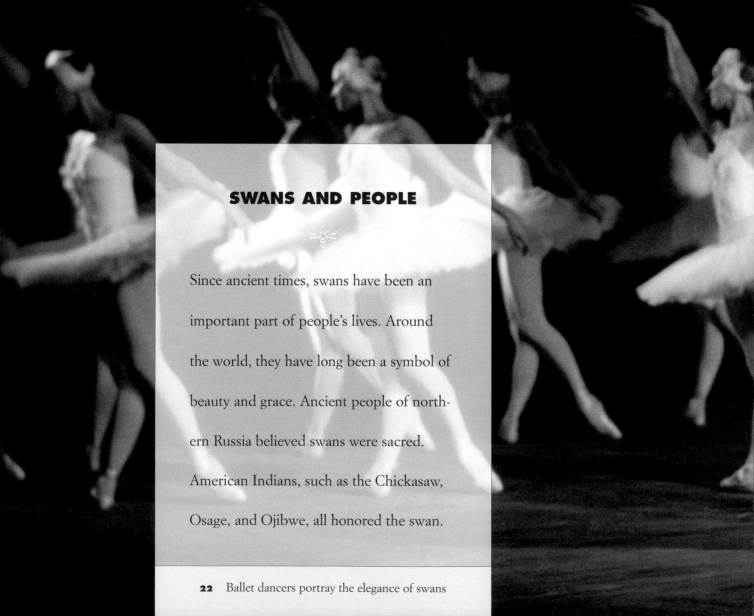

SWANS AND PEOPLE

Since ancient times, swans have been an important part of people's lives. Around the world, they have long been a symbol of beauty and grace. Ancient people of northern Russia believed swans were sacred. American Indians, such as the Chickasaw, Osage, and Ojibwe, all honored the swan.

Ballet dancers portray the elegance of swans

The Iroquois Indians believed that swans
played a part in the creation of the world.
A Greek myth tells about a god who
became a swan. Legends from many **cultures** tell about swans that became human.
A famous ballet called *Swan Lake* tells the
story of a woman who was also a swan.

Swan Lake is performed around the world   **23**

Swans were once a source of food for people. In the north, Native Americans hunted swans by throwing balls of bone at them. They also chased swans across the water and speared them when they were molting and couldn't fly.

In the 1800s, hunters killed many swans. The skins and feathers were used to make

24   English kings once made swans the centerpiece of feasts

hats, powder puffs, and bedding. Swans became scarce in North America until the United States and Canada signed the Migratory Bird Treaty in 1916 to protect migratory birds from **extinction**. After the treaty was passed, tundra swan numbers grew in North America. In the 1960s, hunting became legal again in some areas where swans live.

Swans used to be prized game animals   **25**

Pollution sometimes harms swans. Oil spilled into water can coat their feathers and kill them. Some swans have died from eating lead shot that collects on the bottoms of lakes during hunting season.

Cleaning oil off their feathers can poison swans

Scientists are working to make sure swan populations stay healthy. They **band** swans and put **radio transmitters** on some of them so they can learn more about how, when, and where swans migrate. The information helps wildlife experts understand what swans need to survive and thrive. They can then apply this understanding to making sure human activities don't harm future populations of swans.

28   Fortunately, swan numbers are now on the rise

Today, many people enjoy watching swans. Some tourists travel to places just to see them. Communities around the world hold festivals to celebrate swans. Wherever they are found, swans remind people of the beauty and wonder of our wild world.

The rare trumpeter swan is the largest kind of swan

Adaptations are things about a plant or animal that help it survive where it lives.

Scientists **band** a bird by putting a ring around its leg with information that identifies it.

Cultures are groups of people that share traditions, ideas, and ways of doing things.

The **diameter** of a circular object is the distance from one side to the other through the middle.

Down is the name for the fluffy feathers that cover some baby birds.

Extinction occurs when the last of a certain kind of plant or animal dies.

A **migratory** animal is one that moves from one place to another as the seasons change.

Predators are animals that kill and eat other animals.

Radio transmitters are devices that give off a signal that can be followed from a distance.

Something that is **tapered** is wide at one end and thin or narrow at the other end.

A **trait** is a feature or characteristic of a living or nonliving thing.

BOOKS

Horton, Tim. *Swanfall: Journey of the Tundra Swans*. New York: Walker, 1991.

Lavies, Bianca. *Tundra Swans*. New York: Dutton Children's Books, 1994.

Stone, Lynn. *Swans*. Minneapolis, Minn.: Lerner Publications, 1997.

WEB SITES

Tundra Animals http://mbgnet.mobot.org/sets/tundra/animals/swan.html

EEK! Environmental Education for Kids http://www.dnr.state.wi.us/org/caer/ce/eek/critter/bird/tundraswan.htm

Avian Web: Swans http://www.avianweb.com/swans.htm

INDEX